Born to be Wild

Little Gorillas

Bernadette Costa-Prades

Words that appear in the glossary are printed in
boldface type the first time they occur in the text.

GARETH**STEVENS**
GS

P U B L I S H I N G
A WRC Media Company

One Lucky Baby

What animal spends its day in the forest being cuddled, rocked, and pampered? It's a baby gorilla! A mother gorilla loves playing with her baby, giving it big kisses and tickling the little gorilla to make it laugh. She teaches the baby how to recognize flowers that are good to eat and how to pick fruits. When her little gorilla does something bad, however, she gets angry. When, for example, a baby gorilla disobeys the leader of the gorilla **band**, or family, its mother may scream loudly.

A female gorilla usually has one baby every four or five years. Just after a mother gorilla gives birth, she and her baby are surrounded and protected by all the other gorillas in the family.

What do you think?

How does a mother gorilla carry her baby?

a) She grabs it by the skin on the back of its neck.

b) She carries it in her arms.

c) She carries it under her stomach, where it holds on to her fur.

A mother gorilla carries her baby under her stomach, where it holds on to her fur.

A female gorilla carries her unborn baby inside her body for nine months. After the baby is born, its mother still carries it with her everywhere. For the first six months, the baby holds on to its mother's fur with its hands. When it is strong enough, it climbs onto her back and rides on top of her. It is unusual for a little gorilla to walk on its own until it is two years old. Even then, a little gorilla stays close to its mother.

All the gorillas in a family visit a new baby. They all want to touch it and kiss it. The mother gorilla, however, holds the baby closely to protect it from the noisy activity.

Baby gorillas drink their mother's milk for two years, and they sleep with her until age three — sometimes, even longer!

4

One day, a mother gorilla refuses to feed her baby milk anymore. She no longer wants it to hang onto her or ride on her, either. Even if the little gorilla cries a lot, its mother will not give in. It is her way of saying, "You are a big **ape** now."

Young gorillas love having fun in trees. They swing from branch to branch. As gorillas grow up, they become too heavy to hang from trees so they must stay on the ground.

A Gentle Leader

Gorillas do not like being alone. They always live in a family of ten to twenty members. Each family is led by a chief. The chief is the strongest male in the group. He must protect all the other gorillas in the family and make sure they all get along well. The chief is very patient and gentle with the little gorillas, even when they are being mischievous or loud. When the chief does act grouchy, the little gorillas quiet down right away.

What do you think?

What is the nickname for a gorilla chief?

a) "silverback"

b) the "big noise"

c) "man from the woods"

Gorillas are the biggest of the world's great apes. Along with chimpanzees and orangutans, gorillas are the animals that most resemble humans — especially when they are sitting or standing up.

To become a leader, a male gorilla must be at least fifteen years old. At about this age, the coats of male gorillas become lighter

in color and silvery. The color of the males' coats led to the nickname "silverback." All the other gorillas in a family, from the youngest to the oldest, must obey the **dominant** silverback. He decides each morning where the gorillas will move to next. He also chooses where the band will take naps and where they will sleep at night.

When a band's dominant silverback leaves, another silverback takes its place. Sometimes, after a violent fight, the chief is kicked out of the band by another gorilla. The only thing the loser can do, then, is leave and start another family.

A gorilla chief acts like a protective father. Sometimes, when a mother in the family dies, the chief takes care of her babies himself.

Gorillas love washing one another. They clean each other's fur and pick off itchy bugs. **Grooming** one another is a way gorillas show that they are good friends.

Watch out for the Gorilla!

It is lucky that gorillas are so huge that they do not have many enemies because gorillas do not like fighting. Sometimes, however, a gorilla has to defend itself, but it prefers to scare its enemies away rather than fight them. A gorilla stands up on its back legs and, pounding on its chest with its fists, shouts a terrifying "hoo hoo." If this is not enough to scare an enemy away, the gorilla then starts pulling out grass, throwing leaves up in the air, and running around wildly.

People are the gorilla's only true enemy. People hunt gorillas and either sell them to zoos or eat their meat.

What do you think?

What does a gorilla do when it is annoyed?

a) It throws sand at the head of his enemy.

b) It burps.

c) It goes away.

A gorilla burps when it is annoyed.

Gorillas have a thousand ways to communicate with the other members of their bands. It may not seem like good manners, but when a gorilla is upset, it burps. When it is worried, a gorilla growls. When it is surprised, it barks. To show that they are happy, sad, or afraid, gorillas can make twenty-five different sounds and more than ten expressions and gestures.

A gorilla can throw a terrible tantrum when it is annoyed. Its howls can be heard echoing through the entire forest. A gorilla will suddenly act as if something terrible is about to happen, and then just as quickly, it will calm down.

Few animals are sweeter than gorillas. They never attack unless they are disturbed. When a gorilla does show its teeth, it is because it feels threatened.

Chimpanzees, orangutans, and gorillas, which are known as the great apes, are among the smartest animals in the world. Some of them have even been trained to communicate with people.

No Naps for Little Gorillas

Gorillas are sleepyheads! They spend about half the day napping. Little gorillas, however, don't like sleeping very much. They'd rather be playing in the trees.

What do you think?

Where do gorillas sleep?

a) in nests

b) in caves

c) in holes

When little gorillas make too much noise, they get scolded. If they continue being noisy, they may even get spanked!

Gorillas sleep in nests.

Each night, a gorilla builds a new nest on the ground or, sometimes, in a tree. To build a nest, it needs only a few branches, a thin layer of droppings to **insulate** the nest from the cold ground, and a small pile of fresh leaves for a pillow. Each gorilla builds its own nest, except the youngest gorillas who snuggle against their mothers' warm fur.

Gorillas don't like to travel because it is too tiring for them. They do not normally travel more than about $1/2$ mile (1 kilometer) a day.

Most gorillas build their nests on the ground. When it is stormy or raining heavily, however, they take shelter inside hollow tree trunks.

A little gorilla
learns how to
build a nest by
watching older
family members
build their nests
every evening.
When its mother
is ready to have
another baby,
a young gorilla
will have to build
its nest by itself.

A Leafy Menu

Gorillas are always hungry. They spend most of the day chewing on plants. Sometimes, a gorilla eats up to 45 pounds (20 kilograms) of food in a day. Its menu includes leaves, tender stems, and roots from all kinds of plants. Gorillas also like snails but do not eat them on purpose. Snails just don't have time to get off of a plant that a gorilla is about to eat! Besides earthworms, snails are the only type of meat that gorillas are known to eat.

Because they chew all day long, gorillas often have toothaches. Unfortunately, there aren't any dentists in the forest.

What do you think?

What food does a gorilla like best?

a) **nettles**

b) coconuts

c) bananas

Nettles are a gorilla's favorite food.

Nothing tastes better to a gorilla than a few nettles with thorns! Although gorillas are usually peaceful, they will fight over their favorite food. Nettles are one of the few reasons why gorillas in a band fight. When two gorillas fight over nettles, the chief of the band ends the argument by eating the nettles himself. In addition to these **prickly** plants, gorillas like to eat mushrooms, too.

When gorillas don't have any food, they will eat their own droppings, which are full of vitamins and are very healthy.

Gorillas are so strong that they can pull down a tree to eat the center of it. They peel the bark off, just like peeling a banana, and quietly eat the tender wood inside.

Gorillas rarely drink. The **foliage** they eat contains enough
water, so they don't need to look for more. After it rains,
however, gorillas will lick their wet coats.

Gorillas are **mammals**. They live near the **equator** in the forests of Africa. Mountain gorillas live high in the mountains of Rwanda, and lowland gorillas live on the plains of several African countries. In the wild, gorillas live an average of thirty years. In captivity, they can live up to fifty years. An adult male gorilla weighs between 300 and 500 pounds (140 and 225 kg).

Gorillas are the largest of the primates, which are the most evolved of all animals. Chimpanzees and orangutans are also primates — and so are humans!

A gorilla's thick fur is brown or black. The fur of male gorillas turns silver when they become adults.

Gorillas each have a unique nose print. The folds of their noses help distinguish one gorilla from another.

Gorillas have tiny ears that are almost hidden in their fur.

A gorilla's hands each have four fingers and an **opposable** thumb — just like human hands.

A male gorilla stands 5.5 to 6 feet (168 to 183 centimeters) tall. It is twice as tall as a female gorilla.

A gorilla's feet look the same as its hands.

23

GLOSSARY

ape — one of a group of related mammals, including gorillas, orangutans, and chimpanzees. Apes are large, do not have tails, and can walk upright for short distances.

band — a group of animals or people living or acting together

dominant — having the most power or control

equator — an imaginary line that runs around the middle of Earth, halfway between the North and South Poles

foliage — the leaves of trees and other plants

grooming — cleaning or brushing an animal's coat to keep it neat and free of pests

insulate — to cover, surround, or line with a material that helps keep cold, heat, electricity, or sound from passing through

mammals — warm-blooded animals that have backbones, give birth to live babies, feed their young milk from the mother's body, and have skin that is usually covered with hair or fur

nettles — small plants or bushes with sharp thorns or hairs that cause pain when touched

opposable — able to be placed against one or more of the other fingers or toes on a hand or foot

prickly — having sharp parts, such as thorns

Please visit our web site at: **www.garethstevens.com**
For a free color catalog describing Gareth Stevens Publishing's list of high-quality books and multimedia programs, call **1-800-542-2595** (USA) or **1-800-387-3178** (Canada). Gareth Stevens Publishing's fax: **(414) 332-3567.**

Library of Congress Cataloging-in-Publication Data

Costa-Prades, Bernadette.
[Petit gorille. English]
Little gorillas / Bernadette Costa-Prades. — North American ed.
p. cm. — (Born to be wild)
ISBN 0-8368-4437-8 (lib. bdg.)
1. Gorilla—Infancy—Juvenile literature. I. Title. II. Series.
QL737.P96C67513   2005
599.884'139—dc22   2004059721

This North American edition first published in 2005 by
Gareth Stevens Publishing
A WRC Media Company
330 West Olive Street, Suite 100
Milwaukee, Wisconsin 53212 USA

First published in 2000 as *Le petit gorille* by Mango Jeunesse, an imprint of Editions Mango, Paris, France.

Picture Credits (t = top, b = bottom, l = left, r = right)
BIOS: A. Plumtree 2, 5(tl), 12(tl); M. Harvey 3, 14, 15; M. Gunther 4(r), 16(tl); J. Kalpers/Wildlife 16 (br); S. Turner 21. COLIBRI: A. M Loubsens 8(tl); A. Guerrier 12(br); J. L. Paumard 13, 20 (tr). JACANA: Frédéric 6; M. Willmeit 7; A. Shah & Manoj 18, 19; J. Wegner 22. Phone: C. Jardel/J. M Labat 9. SUNSET: F. Georges cover, title page; Weststock 4(bl); G. Lacz back cover, 5(br), 17, 20(b); D. Cordier 8(br); Animals 10, 23; STF 11.

English translation: Muriel Castille
Gareth Stevens editor: Barbara Kiely Miller
Gareth Stevens art direction: Tammy West

Printed in the United States of America

This U.S. edition copyright © 2005 by Gareth Stevens, Inc.
Original edition copyright © 2000 by Mango Jeunesse.

1 2 3 4 5 6 7 8 9 09 08 07 06 05